# BLACK SANTA

## A SEASON OF JOY

### UMOJA

a trademark of Unity Ink Press LLC

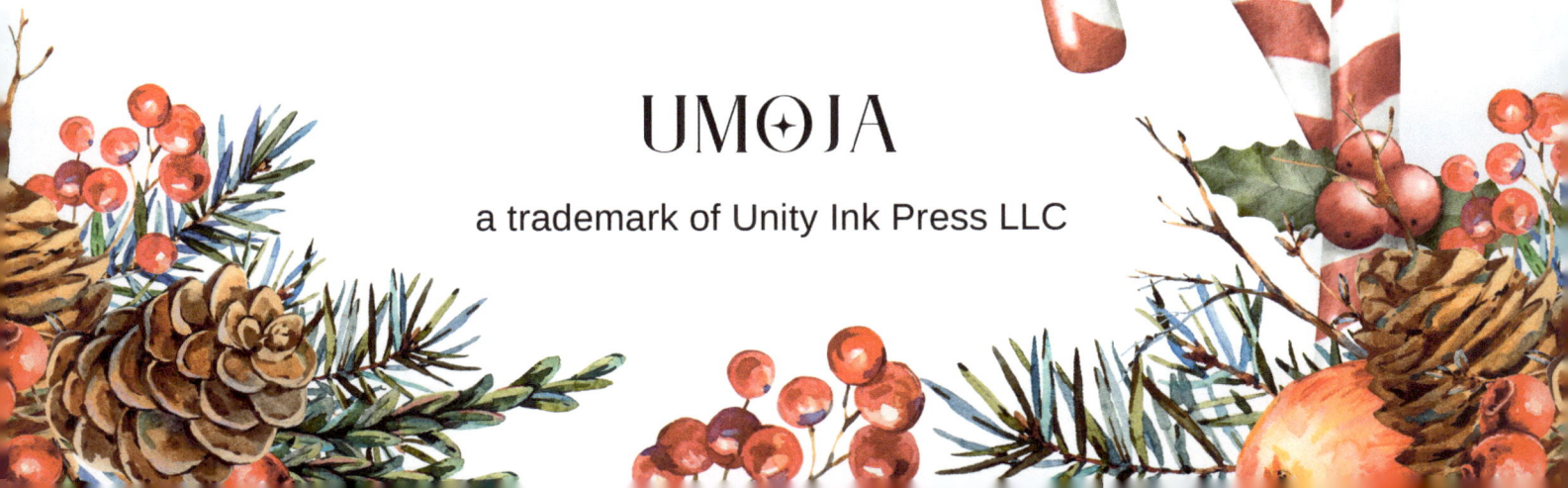

## OFFICIAL LETTER

# BLACK SANTA CLAUS

Dear Queen,

I hope this letter finds you wrapped in peace and surrounded by joy. As the holiday season approaches, I want to remind you of something important - your strength, generosity and spirit does not go unnoticed.

I see the care you pour into your family, friends, work and community. But this season, I'm asking you to do something a little different - take care of you. Don't be afraid to put yourself at the top of your list. You are more than worthy of rest, joy, and time spent savoring the little things that make you smile.

This Christmas, may your days be filled with love and laughter, and may you find warmth not only in the arms of those who love you, but within yourself. You have given so much of yourself all year long - now it's time for you to receive.

With love,

*Black Santa*

May you find joy in your own story, and peace in the chapters you create. Rest, queen, knowing that your story is a *masterpiece.*

Create boldly and dream without limits. The life you envision takes shape through *your hands*, molded by your will and fueled by your passion.

# Standing Tall

Snow falls softly, you stand tall.
On the ranch, you heed the call.
Your boots in snow, gaze steady and bright,
Where you stand, you shine your light.

With grace and strength, you greet each day,
Carving your path, come what may,
Through winter's chill and life's unknown,
You reign as queen on your throne.

So, stand tall, queen, embrace your power,
This is your season; this is your hour.

You're the beat, the bass, the rhythm and soul. The song you create is *beautifully bold*.

Life, like music, is a melody—sometimes soft, sometimes bold, always your own. Every chord you strike, queen, adds to the *song* of your journey.

# At the Table

You rise and attain, with strength in your stride,
Through sunshine and rain, you never hide.
Standing tall, with your spirit so proud,
A light that shines, even through the crowd.

You make bold moves, with wisdom and grace,
Guided by heart, you set the pace.
In boardrooms or life, you lead with flair,
A queen who thrives, no matter where.

You've earned your throne, through trials and fight,
You lead with grace, a beacon of light.
CEO of your dreams, you reign supreme,
Forever the queen, at the helm of your team.

Life is your *masterpiece*, queen – every choice a color, every moment a part of the whole. Paint boldly, and never be afraid to make your mark.

# Crown of Glory

Our hair is protest, our hair is pride,
A declaration we will not hide.
From Afro puffs to locs that sway,
We stand in beauty, come what may.

Hot combs sizzle, braids pull tight,
But each twist, each curl, is a fight—
A fight for freedom, a fight to claim
The right to wear our given mane.

No straightened strand defines our worth,
No box can hold what's birthed from earth.
Our hair tells stories, whispers old,
Of battles won, of strength untold.

Don't be afraid to explore, to test new ideas, and to embrace the wonder of the journey. Sometimes, the greatest *breakthroughs* come from simply believing in the magic of possibility.

# Gliding Through Life

Out on the slopes, carving with ease,
Gliding through powder, catching the breeze.
The trails are steep, but you've got the skills,
Whether black diamonds or bunny hills.

With every turn, with every glide,
I'm here to remind you—enjoy the ride!
Life's a journey, with twists and surprise,
You're flying high, joy lights up your eyes.

From the lift to the lodge, we lead the pack,
Chasing the thrill, we never look back.
So grab your gear, let's embrace the noise—
Life's full of surprises, and endless joys!

# Under the Stars

Beneath the sky, so vast, so wide,
I find peace with you by my side.
In silence, there's beauty, in stillness, grace,
Like the light you carry, you fill every space.

Nature reminds us what we often forget—
To pause, to breathe, to live without regret.

May you always find calm waters, and may your *soul* be full of gratitude, no matter what you catch.

Each sprint has a purpose, each step carries meaning. It's not always about the finish line – it's about giving your all in every run, every challenge, every *dream*.

Life's not about how fast you go. The joy is in the *journey*, not just the end. This season, queen, remember to enjoy the ride.

Santa's lifting more than weights today—he's lifting hope and joy.

You're stronger than you believe, queen. Don't forget to celebrate the *small victories*—they add up to greatness.

# Recipe for Love

## Ingredients:

- 3 cups of patience
- 3 scoops of trust
- A sprinkle of laughter
- A pinch of lust

## Directions:

Step 1: Fold in respect with every turn, and let understanding gently burn.

Step 2: Add in a dash of vulnerability, for love needs truth to grow. Stir in warmth and honesty, and let your heart always show.

Step 3: Let it simmer with time, don't rush the heat. Love, like a fine dish, is a slow, soulful treat.

Step 4: Drizzle with kindness and serve with grace, watch as love lights up your face.

Your hopes and dreams
are planted deep,
waiting for their
moment to rise.

Patience, queen, keep
*watering your soul.* Good
things take time.

# Recipe for Joy

## Ingredients:

- 8 ounces of tranquility
- 1 cup of gratitude
- A handful of smiles
- A scoop of fortitude

## Directions:

Step 1: Pour a dash of acceptance, stirred slow and steady. Fold in forgiveness, let your soul get ready.

Step 2: Let it simmer deep, not just on the surface. Infuse it with light, steep it with purpose

Step 3: Reduce the weight of negativity until it fades. Let the richness of love thicken your gaze.

Step 4: Ask yourself, "Am I worthy of peace?"

*Yes, queen, you are worthy. Now rise and release.*

# *The Cookout*

Smoke in the air, spice on the breeze,
I'm cookin' up joy with a side of ease.
Mac and cheese bubblin', greens in the pot,
Cornbread in the oven, serving love hot.

It's more than the food, it's family and fun,
The stories, the laughter, under the sun.
The grill's just a stage, the flames just for show,
In the company of family, love starts to grow.

# Piece by Piece

Piece by piece, you lay the track,
No map to follow, no looking back.
With steady hands and vision clear,
You shape a journey, year by year.

The landscape shifts, the mountains rise,
Yet you press forward, with open eyes.
No one can see the full design,
But you, conductor, steer the line.

Lay down the rails, firm and true,
Forge your path in all you do.
Piece by piece, your story's made,
A journey rich, that will never fade.

*Invest in yourself*, queen, and watch yourself climb. With each number crunched, with each coin saved, you're building a future that's bold and brave.

Every day offers a new lesson, and you're always a student of life. Keep your mind open, your spirit curious, and remember—*knowledge* is the greatest gift of all.

# Cheers to You!

I'm raising my glass, a twinkle in my eye.
A toast to the queen who reaches for the sky.
With laughter and love, we celebrate tonight,
You've been shining all year, your future is bright.

So here's to the moments, both big and small,
To the times you've stood tall, I noticed it all.
Cheers to your love, passion and grace,
To the strength you carry, the joy on your face.

Raise your glass high, let your spirit be free,
This is your season, as bright as can be.
This toast is to you, full of love and light—
Cheers to your power, your fire, your fight!

When life hands you a *decision* to make, it's important to listen to all sides of the story. Look past the surface to see the deeper truth and trust your judgement.

Every venture brings you closer to the future you make. The code of success is written with grit – keep creating queen. You are destined to win.

You, queen, are like fine wine – *bold* and *complex*. You only get better with the passage of time.

Life, like bread, needs patience to rise. Every ingredient, every step, has its place—just as your joys, challenges, and dreams blend together to make you delectable.

# Joy Ride

We're cruising baby, feeling fine,
You and me, side by side.
It's not the car that's got the flair,
It's you, queen, that's beyond compare.

So let's hit the gas and not hold back,
You've got the drive, keep blazing your track.

Hold your head high, no one else can carry your *crown*. It was made for you.

# Chill and Thrill

Let's chill by the fire,
And savor the thrill,
You're more than just beautiful,
More than just chill.

It's not just your poise,
But the power you show,
Your confidence radiates,
From your head to your toes.

So, own your space,
And claim your throne,
Because sexy is a vibe
That's truly your own.

You're on my *naughty* list. But let's be real— sometimes a little rebellion, a little fire, is exactly what's called for.

Merry Christmas Queen!

www.ingramcontent.com/pod-product-compliance
Lightning Source LLC
Chambersburg PA
CBHW041543260326
41914CB00015B/1535